Carol McNeill

OLD FIFE

A LOOK

First published 2007

ISBN 978-0-9534686-1-4

Published by
Fife Publicity
fifepublicity@ukonline.co.uk

Printed by
Multiprint, Kirkcaldy
Telephone 01592 204755
www.multiprint.tv

Acknowledgements:

Many thanks to Fife Council for their assistance through an
Arts and Heritage Grant, and to Jim Swan and Jim Bell for
the generous loan of their postcards. The remainder of the
illustrations come from the author's postcard collection.

Introduction

The Kingdom of Fife has a rich heritage, with every town and village throughout the county having its own distinctive character and history.

Over the passing of the years, there have been very many changes not only in lifestyle but in the houses, streets and public buildings – many of which have disappeared for ever in the name of progress.

Picture postcards reached the height of their popularity in the early years of the 20th century, when people posted a card in the certainty that it would be delivered later that same day. Using the resources of old postcards, this nostalgic look back at some of the towns and villages in Fife illustrates many of the changes in townscapes and social history. To modern eyes, many of the old buildings were so picturesque that their demolition leaves a sense of loss and frustration. It has to be remembered of course that these simpler living conditions were by no means as idyllic as they appear with hindsight – overcrowding, poor sanitation, earth floors and no electricity would be unacceptable today.

After the Second World War, very many historic buildings were demolished with the aim of providing new and much needed homes, a priority at the time. Over the last few years however, the realisation that our built heritage should be preserved has led to an important change of opinion. This has often been reinforced by the commendable efforts of community and civic groups throughout Fife, who do all they can to make sure that as many old buildings as possible are reprieved, restored and given a new lease of life, allowing the age-old styles to be kept while bringing the interiors up to modern standards.

Many of the scenes pictured here have gone forever, or altered beyond recognition. However, the photographs taken at the time have given us a record of what Fife was like fifty or a hundred years ago, and perhaps will help to encourage an appreciation of our existing heritage which will hopefully remain for future generations.

This image of High Street, Kirkcaldy, was taken around 1912 when trams were a convenient form of transport. John Davidson's stationery shop and business, which published a wide range of picture postcards (including this one) is shown on the left.

An early photograph of the Adam Smith Hall and Beveridge Library which were opened in 1899 by Dunfermline-born Andrew Carnegie. The hall, built with a gallery and magnificent organ, originally had seating for 1300.

Edward Descamps from Belgium posed outside his Kirkcaldy showroom with an early car. His garage and showroom formed part of the Station Hotel building which later became a residential home before being converted into housing.

COMMERCIAL STREET, KIRKCALDY

Commercial Street (formerly Back Street), Kirkcaldy, is pictured in the early 1900s, with Pathhead Hall on the left and refreshment rooms advertising teas and dinners. The curved building on the corner once housed a branch of the Buttercup Dairies.

THE LOCH, BEVERIDGE PARK, KIRKCALDY.

Beveridge Park, gifted to Kirkcaldy by Provost Michael Beveridge, opened in 1892. An ice-cream vendor leaning on his hand cart was just one of the spectators watching the boats on the pond.

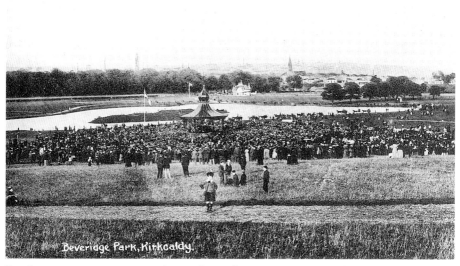

Beveridge Park, Kirkcaldy.

Band concerts were very popular in the early 1900s, as seen in this huge gathering in Beveridge Park. There were several instrumental bands in the town, the most successful being Kirkcaldy Trades Band founded in 1873.

The Docks, Kirkcaldy.

T. G. Blyth, Kirkcaldy

Kirkcaldy harbour was at one time a busy port with a particular importance for the linoleum industry, bringing in cork and shipping out the finished product all over the world.

The Famous Kirk Wynd – Kirkcaldy

Kirk Wynd in Kirkcaldy got its name from the Old Kirk, consecrated in 1244. Writer Thomas Carlyle stayed in the house with the outside stair in 1816 when he taught for two years at the Burgh School, which stood opposite at the junction with Hill Street.

High Street, Kirkcaldy looking East.

A view of the west end of Kirkcaldy High Street shows two church spires – the West End congregational church on the left still stands, while Abbotsrood Church of Scotland closed in 1949.

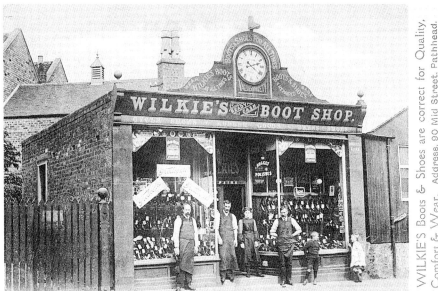

The owner and staff (with two passing children) are pictured outside Wilkie's Boot Shop with its distinctive rooftop clock, in Kirkcaldy's Dunnikier Road. There was another branch of the shop at Pathhead.

Chapel village was a rural hamlet separate from Kirkcaldy when this photograph was taken in 1905. The land originally belonged to the Oswalds of Dunnikier and most of the houses were for agricultural workers.

West Cliff, Kinghorn.   Valentine's Series

Local fishermen are pictured looking across the bay at the row of houses on the seaward side of Kinghorn.

THE BRAES, KINGHORN.

The Braes at Kinghorn were a popular destination for locals and visitors during the summer months, with the small café adding to the attraction.

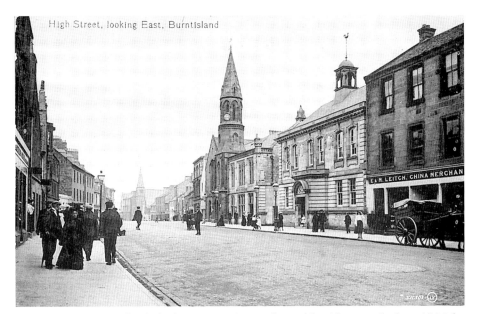

High Street, Burntisland, looking east, shows the public library gifted in 1906 by Andrew Carnegie, and the nearby Town Hall which was built in 1843. Leitch's china merchant is on the right.

Burntisland's High Street was pictured around 1900, with plenty of space for the newly popular bicycles. The horse and cart is delivering to the Green Tree public house.

Aberdour's silver sands made it as popular a place for visitors in 1910 as it is today. Crowds of tourists on a paddle steamer called in at the old stone pier.

A leisurely stroll on the beach at Aberdour was a recognised pastime on a Sunday afternoon, with everyone dressed in their best clothes, including the fine hats worn by the Edwardian ladies.

The view of Dunfermline High Street is dominated by the Gothic-style City Chambers. The electric tram system came to Dunfermline in 1909 and, as in other Fife towns, was welcomed as a cheap and easy form of transport until buses took over in 1937.

Carnegie's Birthplace, Dunfermline.

Andrew Carnegie was born in 1835 in this small cottage in Moodie Street, Dunfermline. One of the world's richest men, he gave huge sums to his home town to improve the quality of people's lives.

The Carnegie Baths opened in 1905, and this image taken in the 1930s shows the pool with changing cubicles at the side as well as a viewing gallery. The building also included Turkish baths, a gymnasium and a billiard room.

High Street, Dunfermline, on a busy afternoon. The front of the tram advertised Dick's Co-operative Institution, popular with shoppers because of its generous dividend to customers.

Andrew Carnegie's most generous gift to Dunfermline was Pittencrieff Estate which he bought in 1902. He wanted the people of the town to enjoy the amenities of the park, including this band kiosk, with its fresh air and relaxation.

Portion of Rosyth Village

Rosyth village – nicknamed Tintown – was built before the First World War to house workers at the dockyard. It was described as a complete community with church, reading room, grocery store and recreational grounds, with low rents.

THE TOWN HALL AND TRON, CULROSS   A 7311

The Town House, just one of the many beautifully preserved old buildings in the conservation village of Culross, was used as the Council Chambers while the ground floor served as the prison.

Bank Street, Lochgelly, is shown around 1905 with horses and carts. The Minto Hotel on the right, which later became a bar, at one time had stables at the back for the guests' horses.

The tram in Lochgelly's Main Street was halted while adjustments were made to the cable. The popular tram service started running in 1909 and was withdrawn in the late 1930s.

Locals posed for the photographer in Lochgelly Main Street in 1903 when horse drawn transport was still the best way to get around. The infamous Lochgelly tawses were made in Robert Philip's shop at the east end of Main Street.

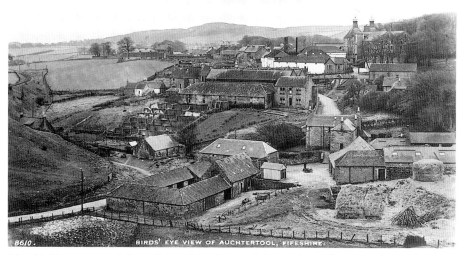

This bird's eye view of the village of Auchtertool shows the maltings in the background as well as farm buildings with traditional hay stacks.

Duchess Lodge and Anderson Hall, Leslie

Duchess Lodge (originally named Countess Lodge) in Leslie marked the outer boundary of Leslie House, once home of the Earls of Rothes. In 1902, ground near the turret subsided revealing a secret room.

Falkland   Valentines Series

The historic village of Falkland was once a favourite of Scottish kings and queens for hunting, hawking and playing tennis at the Palace. The Bruce fountain stands in the square near the Parish Church with the Town Hall in the foreground.

Town Hall, High Street, Dysart.

M. 115

The Tolbooth in Dysart was built in 1576 and incorporated the weights and measures office, guard house and prison. A new Town Hall was built adjoining it in 1887 to mark Queen Victoria's Golden Jubilee, as was the lamp standard at the Cross.

Tall ships brought timber, pantiles, clay and wine to Dysart harbour and left with their holds filled with locally mined coal. A paddle steamer is on the stocks of the shipyard which built and later repaired boats, with the Harbourmaster's House in the background.

Normand Road in Dysart was a quieter place in the 1920s than it is today. The steeple of Normand Road church, built in 1867, is on the left and the primary school is on the right of the picture.

Dysart Cross was bathed in sunshine when this photograph was taken in the 1920s, showing a group of youngsters gathered at the Queen Victoria Jubilee lamp standard. Shops included Forrester the chemist and Owler's newsagents.

St Ser's Tower has dominated the shoreline at Dysart since around the 16th century. The old houses on the shore were completely renovated by the National Trust for Scotland in 1969. The buildings of the Lady Blanche colliery are in the background.

West Wemyss harbour, which dates from the sixteenth century, exported coal from the Victoria and Lady Emma collieries until the early 20th century. With the expansion of Methil docks and the closure of both pits, it fell out of use as a commercial harbour.

The Tolbooth in the High Street at West Wemyss dates back to the early 1700s and was built for David, the fourth Earl of Wemyss. The swan on the weathervane is the symbol of the Wemyss family.

Coxstool, the distinctive building near West Wemyss harbour, was built in the late 1800s as a coffee house to cater for visiting sailors, and was also a reading room for locals.

The children of West Wemyss gathered in the Main Street to have their photograph taken around 1910, with the village policeman keeping an eye on the scene.

Dorothy Sewing School. Coaltown of Wemyss.

The Wemyss School of Needlework in Coaltown of Wemyss was started in 1877 by Lady Dorothy Wemyss, with Jean Webster as the first teacher. Girls were trained in fine sewing and beautiful embroidery, with many orders going to aristocratic families.

Wemyss & District Tramways COALTOWN OF WEMYSS

Wemyss and District Tramway Company was founded by Randolph Wemyss in 1906 and one of the distinctive 'mustard box' tramcars is seen in the main street of Coaltown of Wemyss.

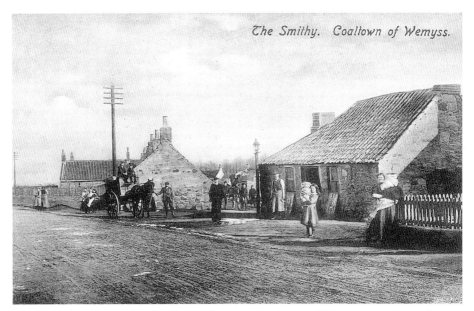

The smithy on the south side of Main Street in Coaltown of Wemyss was a busy place in the early 1900s when horse-drawn transport was the main way to travel. The smith Jack Robertson can be seen at the door with a horseshoe.

This evocative image of Back Dykes in East Wemyss shows the conditions of the day, with horse-drawn transport, gas lights, and the everyday wear of shawl and apron for the women and flat caps for men.

The east end of East Wemyss was called the Brig after the arch in the sea wall which allowed the water of the Back Burn to run into the sea.

Railway staff are pictured at Wemyss Castle station, situated in East Wemyss on a branch line from Thornton to Buckhaven installed by the Wemyss family. There was a special waiting room for guests visiting the castle.

Hawthorn Street in Leven is pictured around 1905. Another of Davidson's postcards, the family in the foreground may have been relatives of the photographer.

The Reform Co-operative Society was on the left of Leven High Street, with Husband the family chemist on the right. The tram service began in 1906.

No trace is left of Links Village, east of Buckhaven. Wemyss Coal Company, which owned Denbeath Colliery (later the Wellesley), rehoused the villagers in Buckhaven and dumped tons of pit waste on the site.

The picturesque old houses on Buckhaven's East Shore, seen here around 1905, were left to dereliction and were demolished in the 1960s. The buildings of the Wellesley Colliery can be seen in the background.

This image of Lower Largo in 1920 shows traditional Fife fishing boats at the old pier, with the railway viaduct and the Crusoe Hotel in the background. Behind is Cardy House, which belonged to the Gillies family, with their net factory which was opened in 1867.

MAIN STREET WEST, UPPER LARGO

The main street at Upper Largo, dating probably from the 1950s, shows the corner garage with the petrol pumps of the day, with a lemonade lorry delivering to a local shop and a single-decker bus picking up passengers.

Keil Burn and Crusoe Hotel, Lower Largo. 6.

Rowing boats are framed by the railway viaduct in front of the Crusoe Hotel, Lower Largo in the 1950s. The hotel was originally a granary, built in 1824. Part of the building was gutted in a fire in 1911 and the hotel was later rebuilt and extended.

Elie High Street is pictured before the First World War, looking east towards the site of the former Toll Bar, with 'Cairter Allen' who had his own carting business in the village. The Clydesdale Bank building is still there although no longer operates as a bank.

The horse drawn vehicle is parked outside the Victoria Hotel in Elie High Street, with the former Burgh School on the other side of School Wynd. The Wood Memorial Church can be seen in the background and the corner shop was Don's the shoemaker.

Elie beach was as popular in Edwardian times as it is today even though seaside fashions have changed. The group of little girls were taking part in the annual Seaside Mission.

This view of Elie from the harbour with local fishing boats includes the old granary on the left of the picture, now converted into housing.

High St.   Earlsferry

M. Wane & Co., Edinbro'. No. 164.

The Royal Burgh of Earlsferry and the Burgh of Elie were at one time two separate villages, and were amalgamated in 1929. This view of Earlsferry High Street was taken around 1910 and shows the Town Hall in the background.

Shore Street East, Anstruther, is pictured with some of the local fishing fleet tied up at the quay. The inner harbour was deepened in 1933 and the harbour wall was widened a few years later.

Dr Andrew Chalmers, the first Moderator of the Assembly of the Free Church of Scotland, was born in 1780 in this cottage in Anstruther High Street. After his family left, it became the Post Office before being taken over by the National Trust for Scotland.

The Chalmers Memorial Lighthouse at Anstruther pier was gifted to the village in 1880 by Hannah Harvey, who also donated a new lifeboat.

Pittenweem harbour is now the busiest of all the East Neuk villages, with a bustling commercial fish market. Many of its old houses have been sensitively restored.

Picturesque Crail harbour is the subject of innumerable paintings and postcards. It is shown here in the early 1900s before many of the old buildings were renovated.

The sands at Roome Bay, Crail, show holiday makers enjoying the beach in the early 1930s with rows of changing huts in the background.

Cupar's Mercat Cross once stood nearer the south side of the Crossgate, and in 1812 it was removed to Tarvit Hill before being brought back into town. The unicorn and shaft were put back on a new base to celebrate Queen Victoria's Diamond Jubilee in 1897.

This view of Crossgate in Cupar was taken in the 1920s and shows horse-drawn carts and gas lamps, with the Mercat Cross in the background and the tower and weathervane of the old Burgh Chambers on the right.

The *Mars*, moored off Newport, was a training ship for boys in trouble with the law or in need of care. Discipline was on strict naval lines and conditions were hard. This picture shows the *Mars* in 1929 on the way to being scrapped at Inverkeithing.

St Andrews harbour is pictured in 1931, with rowing boats available for hire and youngsters trying their hand at fishing off the pier. The Royal George tenement is pictured to the left, with a horse and cart in front of what was then the Bell Rock Tavern.

This view of St Andrews Castle from the south-east also shows the low-water swimming pool which was built in 1904 for lady bathers only. The pavilion for hiring towels and bathing costumes was built under the shelter of the cliffs.

There was a good audience at one of the regular band concerts held at the bandstand (built in 1905) on the Scores. The Martyrs' Monument was erected in 1843 to commemorate the Protestant martyrs of the Reformation.

A putting green was laid out in 1914 on the Bruce Embankment overlooking the bay at St Andrews. Although some locals objected because it would mean moving the stance for the outdoor pierrots, it proved a popular pastime.

South Street, St Andrews, on Market Day.

This image of the annual Lammas Market in South Street around 1910 shows the stalls as well as the wooden living wagons of the showmen who bid for their stances at an onsite auction. Until the First World War it was both a fair and a feeing market.

St. Andrews. South Street

South Street around 1906 is seen on a quieter day than the picture above, with only two horse drawn vehicles. The first of the distinctive lime trees were planted in the street in the early 1880s. The towers of the ruined Cathedral can be seen in the distance.

Donkey rides on the West Sands were a regular entertainment for youngsters during the summer holidays. The donkeys were brought into town to Queen's Gardens as part of the fairground attractions during the Lammas Market.

St. Katharines School, St. Andrews, Fife   *The Playground*

Outdoor activities were part of the curriculum at St Katherine's School (the junior school to St Leonard's), in St Andrews. Schoolgirls posed for a gymnastic display while fellow pupils watered plants in part of the school's garden.

"Joan"

"A. Anderson.
St. Andrews."

Joan Clark wheeled her barrow round the streets of St Andrews until the 1920s selling freshly caught fish. She wore the traditional striped skirt and white apron, red knitted bodice with a shawl, and spotless white stockings with elastic sided boots.

North Street, St. Andrews

North Street, along with the Shorehead, was once the heart of the fishing community in St Andrews, and this 1891 postcard shows some of the fisher folk along with their gear used in baiting the lines.